How
To Be
The

GREATEST
IN GOD'S
KINGDOM

Understanding the Value
Of Servanthood

Byron D. August

Unless otherwise indicated, all scriptural quotations are from the *King James Version* of the Bible.

How To Be the Greatest in God's Kingdom
Understanding the Value of Servanthood
Published by:
Byron D. August
P. O. Box 2833
Broken Arrow, OK 74013
ISBN 0-9673727-0-4

Text Design: Lisa Simpson

Printed in the United States of America.

Contents

Dedication

This book is dedicated to my wife,
Dr. Sylvia August, who has served me faithfully
for the past seven years of marriage.
She is an inspiration to me.
I love her with all my heart.

Acknowledgment

I would like to thank Pastor and Mrs. Kenneth Hagin Jr. for the opportunity to serve at RHEMA Bible Church and Kenneth Hagin Ministries for the past ten years.

Preface

The purpose of this book is to inspire and motivate the Body of Christ to a lifestyle of service. As Christians, we are commanded by our Lord and Savior Jesus Christ to live a life of servanthood. Jesus lived His life in the spirit of excellence, serving mankind even to the point of death. And we should serve others with the same spirit of excellence — not grudgingly, but willingly.

With His servant's heart, Jesus displayed the love of God to mankind. We must follow the same example Jesus set and lay down our lives in service to God. This is how the world will see God's love in us. And this love in us will be a light to those in darkness.

In our modern society, the word "servant" often has a negative connotation. People do not like to think of themselves as servants. To some people, the word "servant" is demeaning and derogatory. I believe this book will change the mentality of anyone who may think "serving" is a bad word.

This book will explain what it means to be a servant and why servanthood is so important to the Body of Christ. We will study three different areas of service: serving in our everyday life, serving in our local church through the ministry of helps, and serving in our workplace. I pray that through this book, you will be inspired and motivated to serve your fellowman with the same love and spirit of excellence that Jesus displayed throughout His life. I hope that just as football players run after a fumbled football, you will be clawing, scratching, and knocking others down, so to speak, running after opportunities to serve people.

Hebrews 6:10 says, *"For God is not unrighteous to forget your work and labour of love, which ye have shewed toward his name, in that ye have ministered to the saints, and do minister."* This verse was written to encourage you to continue serving even when people don't take notice of your effort or deeds. You need to understand that God will never forget your labors of love!

So let us always be about the Father's business — following in the footsteps of Jesus as we serve God by serving people.

CHAPTER 1

The Life of a Servant

Jesus was the greatest Servant who ever walked the earth. He laid down His life for all humanity. And now it is our duty to follow His example and lay down our life for Him. Christ demonstrated the love of God through serving others. Love *requires* serving. In order to truly love, we must *serve*. Just as faith without works is dead (James 2:26), so love without serving is dead. Love requires action.

We will serve the people we love. For illustration, when a person squeezes an orange, he gets orange juice. In the same way, when we squeeze love, serving is what comes out. In other words, loving and serving go hand in hand. They are as closely related as being in water and getting wet. We can't have one without the other.

Christ's love for man motivated Him to endure death on the Cross. Jesus' death was His ultimate act of serving, and His love for us motivated Him to do it. Now our love for Him motivates us to serve mankind. If we truly love God, we will serve His children.

The word translated "serve" in the New Testament is the Greek word "diakoneo" which means *to minister*. Of course, we can minister to people in many different ways. When most people think of ministry, they think of preaching or teaching. But according to the Bible, we minister to people by serving them.

To me, to serve means *to work.* The first thing I learned in Bible school was that ministry is spelled w-o-r-k. Those who don't like to work are usually going to have problems in life, especially if they believe they have been called to the fivefold ministry. It's important to realize that being in the ministry is all about serving and helping people.

When I was a child, my grandmother told me that hard work keeps a man young. I am finding that to be true. But we shouldn't work hard just to keep ourselves young. As Christians, we should work hard, striving to be the best at everything we do. It doesn't matter in what area we serve. In our everyday lives, in our local churches, and in our careers or ministries, we should serve from the heart. And our serving should be done with excellence.

Jesus brought joy and happiness to many people by serving them. We should endeavor to do the same by laying down our lives for each other.

JOHN 15:12,13
12 This is my [Jesus'] commandment, That ye love one another, as I have loved you.
13 Greater love hath no man than this, that a man lay down his life for his friends.

In Luke chapter 10, Jesus mentioned one of the greatest acts of serving found in the Word of God. It is usually referred to as the story of the Good Samaritan. We can learn valuable lessons from this story.

LUKE 10:29-37

29 But he [a certain lawyer], **willing to justify himself, said unto Jesus, And who is my neighbour?**

30 **And Jesus answering said, A certain man went down from Jerusalem to Jericho, and fell among thieves, which stripped him of his raiment, and wounded him, and departed, leaving him half dead.**

31 **And by chance there came down a certain priest that way: and when he saw him, he passed by on the other side.**

32 **And likewise a Levite, when he was at the place, came and looked on him, and passed by on the other side.**

33 **But a certain Samaritan, as he journeyed, came where he was: and when he saw him, he had compassion on him,**

34 **And went to him, and bound up his wounds, pouring in oil and wine, and set him on his own beast, and brought him to an inn, and took care of him.**

35 **And on the morrow when he departed, he took out two pence, and gave them to the host, and said unto him, Take care of him; and whatsoever thou spendest more, when I come again, I will repay thee.**

36 **Which now of these three, thinkest thou, was neighbour unto him that fell among the thieves?**

37 **And he said, He that shewed mercy on him. Then said Jesus unto him, Go, and do thou likewise.**

Because the Good Samaritan had mercy and compassion on the injured man, he went out of his way to help him. We could say he went the "extra mile" and beyond! It has been said that there are never any traffic jams on the extra-mile highway. And that is certainly true when it comes to serving. When the man Jesus was talking to commented on the Good Samaritan's act of kindness, Jesus told him to "Go and do likewise" (v. 37). We should be "doing likewise" today as well.

For many people, it is easier to give some of their money than it is to give of their time. The Good Samaritan gave of his money *and* his time to help the injured man. He bandaged him up and gave him a ride to a nearby hotel. He checked him into the hotel and took care of him through the night. In the morning, he paid for the man's hotel expenses and told the host of the hotel to take further care of the man. He also told the host that he would reimburse him if any expenses exceeded the amount of money he had given him at the start.

As Christians, we should go on a manhunt, so to speak, looking for opportunities to help hurting people. When we have a servant's heart, people will see Jesus in our actions. I once heard a preacher say, "I would rather *see* a sermon than *hear* a sermon," and I think most people would say the same thing! Christians are to be living epistles to the world (2 Cor. 3:3). So we cannot afford to let opportunities to serve people pass us by. The Good Samaritan in Luke chapter 10 walked in the love of God and did not miss the chance to do a good deed for someone in need.

Woe to us when we don't help someone whom we could help. First John 3:17 says, *"But whoso hath this world's good, and seeth his brother have need, and shutteth up his bowels of compassion from him, how dwelleth the love of God in him?"* If we pass by people who need help without doing what we can to help them, does the love of God really dwell in us? We should take advantage of each opportunity to serve that comes our way. Just as a man pursues the woman he is madly in love with, so should we pursue opportunities to serve one another.

A Willing Heart

When we serve people, it's important that we do so with a willing heart. My pastor always says that if a person is going to do something, he or she should do it right the first time. To serve the right way, we should serve with joy and gladness in our heart. Some of the happiest people I know are those who are always being a blessing to others. Regardless if it is a family member, friend, brother or sister in the Lord, or a coworker, it is a joy to serve people — especially the people of God (Gal. 6:10).

There is no greater joy than the joy received from being a blessing to someone. We can serve and bless people in many different ways. We can bless people by cooking a meal for them, cleaning their home, or by laying hands on them in prayer and believing God for healing. It does not matter what we do — whether it be done in the natural realm or the spiritual realm — when we serve with a willing heart, it is a blessing to people.

As Christians, we know that Jesus has set us free, but we need to understand the *purpose* for our liberty. The Bible tells us that we have been set free to serve one another. Galatians 5:13 says, *"For, brethren, ye have been called unto liberty; only use not liberty for an occasion to the flesh, but by love serve one another."* We must strive to walk in the liberty Christ obtained for us by serving those around us with a willing heart and an attitude of love.

The Greatest Servant of All

Jesus is without a doubt the greatest Servant of all. Because of the life He lived and the ultimate act of servanthood He demonstrated on the Cross, mankind is able to be born again. God loves the world so much that He sent His Only Son to serve mankind by dying on the Cross for our sins. We saw God's love manifested in the way Jesus served — in His life and in His death. There is no greater love than to lay down one's life for his fellowman (John 15:13). Jesus humbled Himself and was willing to serve us by laying down His life, and God highly exalted him.

PHILIPPIANS 2:5-11 (*The Living New Testament*)

5   Your attitude should be the kind that was shown us by Jesus Christ,

6   Who, though He was God, did not demand and cling to His rights as God,

7   But laid aside His mighty power and glory, taking the disguise of a slave and becoming like men.

8   And he humbled Himself even further, going so far as actually to die a criminal's death on a cross.

9   Yet it was because of this that God raised Him up to the heights of heaven and gave Him a name which is above every other name,

10 That at the name of Jesus every knee shall bow in heaven and on earth and under the earth,

11 And every tongue shall confess that Jesus Christ is Lord, to the glory of God the Father.

Jesus' death on the Cross was the greatest act of love and service ever displayed. That act of service motivated me to become a Christian. When I discovered the price Jesus paid for me, I gave my life to Him.

Whenever a person makes a notable sacrifice, it is inspiring, and it touches the hearts of those around him. For example, when a baseball player gives all he has diving to catch a line drive, it inspires and motivates his teammates to give all they have. It helps them to know he would sacrifice his body for the good of the team. In the same way, when we sacrifice our talents and time to show the love of God to the lost, it inspires and motivates them to come to Christ.

Serving Has Its Benefits

There are many benefits to living as a servant. I have heard many testimonies of people who were healed or had their need met while they were helping another person. God is not a respecter of persons (Acts 10:34). What He does for one person, He will do for another.

When we take our mind off our problems and start helping and serving others, God always meets our needs. A good example of this is the story of the widow woman who served the prophet Elijah in First Kings chapter 17.

1 KINGS 17:9-16

9 Arise, get thee to Zarephath, which belongeth to Zidon, and dwell there: behold, I have commanded a widow woman there to sustain thee.

10 So he arose and went to Zarephath. And when he came to the gate of the city, behold, the widow woman was there gathering of sticks: and he called to her, and said, Fetch me, I pray thee, a little water in a vessel, that I may drink.

11 And as she was going to fetch it, he called to her, and said, Bring me, I pray thee, a morsel of bread in thine hand.

12 And she said, As the Lord thy God liveth, I have not a cake, but an handful of meal in a barrel, and a little oil in a cruse: and, behold, I am gathering two sticks, that I may go in and dress it for me and my son, that we may eat it, and die.

13 And Elijah said unto her, Fear not; go and do as thou hast said: but make me thereof a little cake first, and bring it unto me, and after make for thee and for thy son.

14 For thus saith the Lord God of Israel, The barrel of meal shall not waste, neither shall the cruse of oil fail, until the day that the Lord sendeth rain upon the earth.

15 And she went and did according to the saying of Elijah: and she, and he, and her house, did eat many days.

16 And the barrel of meal wasted not, neither did the cruse of oil fail, according to the word of the Lord, which he spake by Elijah.

Because the widow obeyed God's command to sustain Elijah, God met her need. When she humbled herself and served the man of God, God took care of her. And she is no exception. God *always* takes care of His people. Verse 15 says that she and her house had enough to eat for many days. She put the man of God's needs before her own, and she became the beneficiary of her actions.

That is a biblical principle that applies to us today. When we put God's Kingdom and His commands first, everything else in our life will fall into place. Matthew 6:33 says it best: *"But seek ye first the kingdom of God, and his righteousness; and all these things shall be added unto you."*

Serving in Marriage

The same principle of service that we have been studying applies in the marriage relationship. According to the Bible, husbands should lay down their lives in service to their wives. If husbands would only love their wives the way Christ loves the Church, there would be fewer problems in marriages. The reason why most wives won't cooperate with their husbands is their husbands are not loving them the way they should be. If we men would be a little less selfish, our wives would probably cooperate more with us!

Ephesians 5:25 says, *"Husbands, love your wives, even as Christ also loved the church, and gave himself for it."* In other words, men, we must endeavor to serve our wives just as Christ served the Church. He gave Himself for the Church. He willingly laid down His life for her. And when we lay down our lives for our wives, then our marriages can and will be what God intended for them to be.

EPHESIANS 5:28,29

28 So ought men to love their wives as their own bodies. He that loveth his wife loveth himself.

29 For no man ever yet hated his own flesh; but nourisheth and cherisheth it, even as the Lord the church.

If men would treat their wives the way they themselves want to be treated, there would be more happy marriages in this world. The solution is simple. Husbands, we should go the extra mile in serving our wives. Our wives should feel as though they are the queens of their castles, and we should make their lives easier by waiting on them, or *serving* them.

1 PETER 3:7 (*The Living New Testament*)

7 You husbands must be careful of your wives, being thoughtful of their needs and honoring them as the weaker sex. Remember that you and your wife are partners in receiving God's blessings, and if you don't treat her as you should, your prayers will not get ready answers.

It takes a humble man to serve his wife. Some men think their wives should love *them* the way Christ loves the Church, but the Lord placed that responsibility on the husband. He commanded husbands to love their wives. When we love our wives the way we are supposed to, they will in turn honor us.

You see, serving always precedes honor. When husbands take their proper role in the marriage relation-

ship, then their wives will want to do their part. It is
the responsibility of the husband to keep peace in the
home. I say that because husbands are the ones commanded to love. Husbands are to be the peace*makers*
and the peace*keepers* in marriage. And when a man
serves his wife the way Christ serves the Church, then
his marriage will be a blessing to him and to his wife.

1 CORINTHIANS 13:4,5 (*The Living New Testament*)
    **4   Love is very patient and kind, never jeal-
ous or envious, never boastful or proud,**
    **5   Never haughty or selfish or rude. Love
does not demand its own way. It is not irritable
or touchy. It does not hold grudges and will
hardly even notice when others do it wrong.**

Let me offer a side thought on the importance of
being willing to love and serve. If a man cannot love his
wife the way Christ loves the Church, he should certainly not pursue being in the ministry, because ministry is all about loving and serving people.

How To Be Great in God's Kingdom

If you want to be great in God's Kingdom, humility
is a must! The greatest leaders in the Bible were those
who were humble before God and man. Another word
for "humble" is "meek." Moses is an excellent example
of a meek man whom God made great.

NUMBERS 12:3
    **3   (Now the man MOSES WAS VERY MEEK,
above all the men which were upon the face of
the earth.)**

Meekness is one of the fruits of the Spirit (Gal. 5:23). Being meek allows God to open the door of promotion and blessing in our lives. If we humble ourselves and let the Lord use us as He sees fit, we will not have to be concerned with getting our needs met. We must decrease and let the Lord increase in our lives (John 3:30). When we allow this transition to take place, God can move us up and promote us.

LUKE 14:11

11 For whosoever exalteth himself shall be abased; and he that humbleth himself shall be exalted.

God's ways and the world's ways are totally opposite one another. The Kingdom of God and the world's system are completely different. God says to *give*; the world says to *get all you can get*. God's way is to *serve*; the world's way is to *be served*.

If we want to be a successful in both our natural and spiritual life, we must follow God's way of doing things. That means we must humble ourselves and serve. Jesus humbled Himself and served, and God exalted Him both naturally and spiritually.

1 JOHN 3:16

16 Hereby perceive we the love of God, because he [Jesus] laid down his life for us: and we ought to lay down our lives for the brethren.

We know and understand God's love through Jesus' death on the Cross. Jesus is our example and motivation for loving and serving mankind. Serving is an outward expression of what is in our heart. Serving is love in demonstration. A person who walks in the love of

God is a servant of God. And if we want to be great in the Kingdom of God, we must learn to serve people.

MATTHEW 23:11,12
11 But he that is greatest among you shall be your servant.
12 And whosoever shall exalt himself shall be abased; and he that shall humble himself shall be exalted.

The Bible says that if you want to be great in God's Kingdom, then you have to serve. You have to lay down your life — your plans and desires — to serve people. That is how you will become great in God's eyes and receive true blessings.

The United States of America is said to be the greatest country in the world. As a nation, we surpass other countries economically, socially, and medically. We have arguably the best military force in the world. We also have an abundance of food, clothing, and other materials.

Often when there is a crisis in the world, the United States is the first country to respond to the needs of people. We send planes loaded with food, clothing, and medical supplies to the place of devastation. We also send people to serve in different capacities. This country as a whole has the reputation of serving. Our willingness to serve is one of the reasons why our nation has been so blessed.

ACTS 20:35
35 I have shewed you all things, how that so labouring ye ought to support the weak, and to remember the words of the Lord Jesus, how he said, It is more blessed to give than to receive.

From this verse of Scripture, we could say that it is also more blessed to be a servant than it is to be served. But there is a definite reward for serving. We know from God's Word that whatever a person sows is what he will reap (Gal. 6:7). Therefore, we can rest assured that when we serve, we will also be served. We will always reap what we sow.

CHAPTER 2

Serving God by Serving People

If we want to touch the heart of God, we need to serve people. God has always been and will always be interested in people. And we serve God best by serving people.

MATTHEW 25:35-40

35 For I was an hungred, and ye gave me meat: I was thirsty, and ye gave me drink: I was a stranger, and ye took me in:

36 Naked, and ye clothed me: I was sick, and ye visited me: I was in prison, and ye came unto me.

37 Then shall the righteous answer him, saying, Lord, when saw we thee an hungred, and fed thee? or thirsty, and gave thee drink?

38 When saw we thee a stranger, and took thee in? or naked, and clothed thee?

39 Or when saw we thee sick, or in prison, and came unto thee?

40 And the King shall answer and say unto them, Verily I say unto you, Inasmuch as ye have done it unto one of the least of these my brethren, ye have done it unto me.

Most people can tell how a Christian really feels about God by the way he or she treats other people. First John 4:20 says, *"If a man say, I love God, and hateth his brother, he is a liar: for he that loveth not his brother whom he hath seen, how can he love God whom he hath not seen?"* In other words, the way we treat our fellowman is a direct reflection of our love for the Lord.

When we mistreat a brother in Christ, we are mistreating God. When we slander a sister in Christ, we are slandering God. When we discriminate against someone because of his race, we are discriminating against God.

Someone might argue this fact and say it isn't true. But I didn't make it up. It's what the Bible says. Saul, who became the Apostle Paul, was on his way to Damascus when he discovered that all the time he had been persecuting Christians, he had been persecuting Christ.

ACTS 9:3-5
3   And as he [Paul] journeyed, he came near Damascus: and suddenly there shined round about him a light from heaven:
4   And he fell to the earth, and heard a voice saying unto him, Saul, Saul, why persecutest thou me?
5   And he said, Who art thou, Lord? And the Lord said, I am Jesus whom thou persecutest: it is hard for thee to kick against the pricks.

Jesus asked Paul why he was persecuting Him. Paul had never met Jesus in person. Paul was persecuting Christians, and Jesus took it personally. In the same way, every time we hurt or injure a brother or sister in the Lord, we are hurting or injuring the Lord Jesus Himself.

As I said earlier, we should be practically "knocking each other down" to serve one another. Galatians 6:10 says, *"As we have therefore opportunity, let us do good unto all men, especially unto them who are of the household of faith* [the Body of Christ]." We should take advantage of each opportunity we have to do good and serve our brothers and sisters in the Lord.

But we should also love and serve those outside the Body of Christ.

ROMANS 12:9,10
9   Let love be without dissimulation. Abhor that which is evil; cleave to that which is good.
10 Be kindly affectioned one to another with brotherly love; in honour preferring one another.

We must always seek the best for one another and go out of our way to help others. It is important that we be prepared to serve. In Acts chapter 9, Ananias was ready and willing to serve when the Lord needed him. And in spite of the rumors he had heard about Saul, Ananias helped Saul because of his own love for God. Like Ananias, we should always be ready to assist, give, and serve at a moment's notice.

Doing Good and
Destroying the Devil's Work

Let's look at the story about Jairus in Mark chapter 5. Jairus' daughter was at the point of death, so he asked Jesus to go to his house and lay His hands on her that she may be healed.

MARK 5:22-24

22 And, behold, there cometh one of the rulers of the synagogue, Jairus by name; and when he saw him [Jesus], he fell at his feet,

23 And besought him greatly, saying, My little daughter lieth at the point of death: I pray thee, come and lay thy hands on her, that she may be healed; and she shall live.

24 And Jesus went with him; and much people followed him, and thronged him.

Notice that Jesus did not tell Jairus that He couldn't go to his house that day because He was busy hanging out with His disciples. No, Jesus had compassion on Jairus. Jesus went to Jairus' home, laid His hands on his daughter, and she was made well (v. 41,42).

Jesus did a good thing for Jairus that day. The Bible tells us that when Jesus walked the earth, He went around doing good things for people.

ACTS 10:38

38 How God anointed Jesus of Nazareth with the Holy Ghost and with power: who WENT ABOUT DOING GOOD, and healing all that were oppressed of the devil; for God was with him.

In His earthly ministry, Jesus was a blessing everywhere He went. The power of God flowed through Jesus' life and ministry regardless of His location. Jesus healed the sick, cast out devils, and worked miracles. God manifested Himself through Jesus on the coastlines, in the mountains, in houses, and in synagogues.

In serving people, Jesus was destroying the devil's work. That's what Jesus came to earth to do. First John 3:8 says, *"He that committeth sin is of the devil; for the devil sinneth from the beginning. For this purpose the Son of God was manifested, that he might destroy the works of the devil."* Sin, sickness, disease, and poverty are all the works of the devil, which Jesus destroyed through serving people.

As followers of Jesus, we should pick up where He left off. In John 14:12, Jesus said, *"Verily, verily, I say unto you, He that believeth on me, the works that I do shall he do also; and greater works than these shall he do; because I go unto my Father."* We shall do these greater acts of service when we pursue the plans and purposes of God for our lives. God wants to use us to minister to people in the same way He used Jesus to minister to people. Not everyone is called to the fivefold ministry, but we can all serve people in some way.

Keeping Your Heart Focused on People

When we serve people, we are laying up treasures in Heaven. We should always stay rich in doing good deeds for others.

MATTHEW 6:19-21
19 Lay not up for yourselves treasures upon earth, where moth and rust doth corrupt, and where thieves break through and steal:

20 But lay up for yourselves treasures in heaven, where neither moth nor rust doth corrupt, and where thieves do not break through nor steal:

21 For where your treasure is, there will your heart be also.

Verse 21 tells us that where we store up our treasure is where our heart will be. Whatever our mind thinks about most reveals where our heart is. For example, do you remember your first love? You thought about that person every second of the day, because your heart was with them. We should have a heart for people. Our hearts should remained focused on loving and serving people.

In the church I attended nearly twenty years ago, the pastor made an announcement every other week for volunteers to work at the church. There were two men who always raised their hand. I never saw them without smiles on their faces. They were always willing to help and serve in any way possible.

Some church members who were unwilling to serve even went so far as to tell the pastor that they needed to pray first about coming over to help. Others would claim a sudden bad back, knee, or shoulder. These people thought it was the pastor's responsibility to do all the preaching *and* all the work. But watching the Lord bless the ones who were willing to serve inspired me to want to serve.

We never know who is watching us and the way we live. That is why it is important that our lives always be a living testimony of serving. As Christians, we should never be called lazy, but we should always be busy doing something profitable. Titus 3:8 says, *"This is a faithful saying, and these things I will that thou affirm constantly, that THEY WHICH BELIEVED IN GOD MIGHT BE CAREFUL TO MAINTAIN GOOD WORKS. These things are good and profitable unto men."* This verse plainly tells us that *good works* are profitable unto men.

Biblical Examples of Servanthood

In John chapter 13, Jesus gives us an excellent example of servanthood in action.

JOHN 13:4-10,12-15

4 He [Jesus] riseth from supper, and laid aside his garments; and took a towel, and girded himself.

5 After that he poureth water into a bason, and began to wash the disciples' feet, and to wipe them with the towel wherewith he was girded.

6 Then cometh he to Simon Peter: and Peter saith unto him, Lord, dost thou wash my feet?

7 Jesus answered and said unto him, What I do thou knowest not now; but thou shalt know hereafter.

8 Peter saith unto him, Thou shalt never wash my feet. Jesus answered him, If I wash thee not, thou hast no part with me.

9 Simon Peter saith unto him, Lord, not my feet only, but also my hands and my head.

10 Jesus saith to him, He that is washed needeth not save to wash his feet, but is clean every whit: and ye are clean. . . .

12 So after he had washed their feet, and had taken his garments, and was set down again, he said unto them, Know ye what I have done to you?

13 Ye call me Master and Lord: and ye say well; for so I am.

14 If I then, your Lord and Master, have washed your feet; ye also ought to wash one another's feet.

15 For I have given you an example, that ye should do as I have done to you.

Using a vivid object lesson, Jesus taught His disciples something very important concerning the subject of serving. In verse 14, He said, "If I, your Lord and Master, wash *your* feet, all of you should wash *each other's* feet." Jesus was really saying, "Since I have been a servant unto each of you, you should each be servants to one another." In this simple lesson, Jesus taught us that no one is too good to serve. It does not matter how much money a person makes or how successful he is in the corporate world. Jesus served, so we can serve. In God's eyes, no one is too important to serve His people.

Many people today are seeking popularity and fame. They want to be seen by people. They don't understand that with God the way up is down. In other words, when we humble ourselves, God will exalt us above and beyond anything we can imagine.

Dorcas

In Acts 9:36, we read about a sister in Joppa who was full of good works and busy serving the people of the city.

ACTS 9:36
36 Now there was at Joppa a certain disciple named Tabitha, which by interpretation is called Dorcas: this woman was full of good works and almsdeeds which she did.

Dorcas was a blessing to many of the people in Joppa. She used her talents and gifts to bless people.

Dorcas' talent was in the area of sewing. The Bible says she made coats and garments for the people of Joppa.

ACTS 9:39
39 Then Peter arose and went with them. When he was come, they brought him into the upper chamber: and all the widows stood by him weeping, and shewing the coats and garments which Dorcas made, while she was with them.

Whatever the Lord has anointed and blessed *you* to do, do it with joy. Love can be expressed in so many different ways, such as cutting grass, cooking, cleaning, praying, or giving someone a ride to work. Discover your talent, and be a blessing where you are. A great place to start is right in your own home. Yet sometimes it is difficult to serve the people we live with because they often take us for granted, but if we endeavor to be a blessing to them, God will bless us.

Cornelius

Cornelius was another servant in the Early Church who was a blessing to those around him.

ACTS 10:1-4 (*The Living New Testament*)
1   In Caesarea there lived a Roman army officer, Cornelius, a captain of an Italian regiment.
2   He was a godly man, deeply reverent, as was his entire household. He gave generously to charity and was a man of prayer.

3 While wide awake one afternoon he had a vision — it was about three o'clock — and in this vision he saw an angel of God coming toward him. "Cornelius!" the angel said.

4 Cornelius stared at him in terror. "What do you want, sir?" he asked the angel. And the angel replied, "Your prayers and charities have not gone unnoticed by God!"

Evidently Cornelius was a prosperous man. The Bible says he gave generously to the poor. Cornelius served people with his finances and with his prayers. In verse 4, the angel of the Lord told Cornelius that his prayers and his giving had not gone unnoticed by the Lord. All Cornelius' giving was to people, but God knew about it.

You see, when we serve God's people, God knows about it. Because Cornelius had a heart after God, he gave of his earthly goods. Then God blessed him with spiritual goods. Remember, when we do good deeds, God is always keeping tabs.

PSALM 41:1

1 Blessed is he that considereth the poor: the Lord will deliver him in time of trouble.

TITUS 2:14

14 [Jesus] Who gave himself for us, that he might redeem us from all iniquity, and purify unto himself a peculiar people, zealous of good works.

We should be a people zealous to do good works. Let it never be said that we allowed an opportunity to be a blessing to someone pass us by.

CHAPTER 3

Serving in the Local Church

T he people who serve in the helps ministry are a vital part of the Body of Christ, and they should never be taken for granted. Without the ministry of helps, the fivefold ministry would be in serious trouble. The Lord's disciples served in the ministry of helps. And if Jesus needed help in His ministry, the men and women in fivefold-ministry offices today need our help! Many pastors try to do everything on their own. They should let the Lord raise up people in their ministries to be a blessing to them and to the local church.

> **1 CORINTHIANS 12:28**
> **28 And God hath set some in the church, first apostles, secondarily prophets, thirdly teachers, after that miracles, then gifts of healings, HELPS, governments, diversities of tongues.**

The helps ministry was designed by God to be a blessing to the Body of Christ. The Greek word translated "helps" in this verse is "antilepsis" which means *to lay hold of in order to support.* The helps ministry is just as anointed as any other of the ministry offices.

Because of all that ministers of helps do in the Body of Christ, the fivefold ministers are able to be more of a blessing to the people. You see, it would be very difficult for the pastor of a church to preach and for the people in the congregation to receive if the pastor had to leave the pulpit in the middle of his sermon to go work in the nursery or in the parking lot. This is one example of why the helps ministry is vital to the Body of Christ.

The Importance of Being Impartial

When visitors come to church, the first people they come in contact with are most likely those involved in the helps ministry. Parking lot attendants, greeters, and ushers must always be on their toes, so to speak, and always be led by the Spirit of God. It could make the difference in whether or not a person accepts Christ. Therefore, we should greet everyone with a warm welcome and a nice, friendly smile — regardless of the person's looks, clothes, or hairstyle.

God loves people. So when we deal with people, we must remember that each one is valuable. We should treat everyone with respect, regardless of race, color, or nationality. And we should be willing to serve everyone.

JAMES 2:2-4
2 For if there come unto your assembly a man with a gold ring, in goodly apparel, and there come in also a poor man in vile raiment;
3 And ye have respect to him that weareth the gay clothing, and say unto him, Sit thou here in a good place; and say to the poor, Stand thou there, or sit here under my footstool:

4 Are ye not then partial in yourselves,
and are become judges of evil thoughts?

Man looks on the outward appearance. God looks at
the heart of people. As children of God, we should look
at people the same way God does.

Remember, we are called to serve *all* people. Jesus
did not show favoritism; He helped everyone who came
to Him. And we need to follow His example by helping
everyone who comes to us.

Everyone Has a Part to Play

It is vitally important for each person who serves in
the helps ministry to know his or her individual role.
Let me illustrate that point. For example, on a basket-
ball team there are two guards, two forwards, and one
center. While one player may be good at dribbling the
ball down the court, another may be good at shooting
baskets, while still another may be good at getting
rebounds. The fourth member of the team may play
great defense, and the fifth member may be good at
blocking shots. Although each player is good individu-
ally at a certain skill, the goal is for everyone to play
together as a team.

In the same way, the helps ministry is a team effort.
Everyone involved must work together while at the
same time doing what each one does best.

According to the Bible, anything can be accomplished when all parties involved are in agreement and
unity. In Genesis chapter 11, we see the power of unity
in demonstration during the construction of the Tower
of Babel.

GENESIS 11:1-6

1 And the whole earth was of one language, and of one speech.

2 And it came to pass, as they journeyed from the east, that they found a plain in the land of Shinar; and they dwelt there.

3 And they said one to another, Go to, let us make brick, and burn them thoroughly. And they had brick for stone, and slime had they for morter.

4 And they said, Go to, let us build us a city and a tower, whose top may reach unto heaven; and let us make us a name, lest we be scattered abroad upon the face of the whole earth.

5 And the Lord came down to see the city and the tower, which the children of men builded.

6 And the Lord said, Behold, the people is one, and they have all one language; and this they begin to do: and now nothing will be restrained from them, which they have imagined to do.

God said nothing would be impossible for the people because they were all of one mind and one accord. God had to confuse their language to stop them from accomplishing what they planned to do. This shows the power in unity. There is power when each member of the Body of Christ is serving God in his or her own position.

Unity is a vital ingredient in the helps ministry. Amos 3:3 asks, *"Can two walk together, except they be agreed?"* Everyone involved in the area of helps should know the vision of his pastor or leader. It's just as important for a minister of helps to know who is the head of the ministry as it is for a team to know who the coach is. It makes playing your position a whole lot easier!

Pray for Your Pastor

The pastor and those in the helps ministry should flow together in unity at *all* times. In other words, if the pastor wants something done one way, and I think it should be done another way, then I must submit to my pastor, do it his way, and pray about the situation. Unfortunately, many church members end up causing more problems by talking negatively about the situation and their pastor. They should never speak negatively about the pastor or those in authority over them. Christians can get more accomplished by spending time in prayer over a situation than by talking about it with everyone in the church.

1 TIMOTHY 2:1,2
1   I exhort therefore, that, first of all, supplications, prayers, intercessions, and giving of thanks, be made for all men;
2   For kings, and for all that are in authority; that we may lead a quiet and peaceable life in all godliness and honesty.

This passage reminds us that we have a responsibility to pray for our pastors and for all those in authority over us.

Maximize Your Potential by
Doing Your Part

When serving in the local church in the ministry of helps, it is very important to stay in your area of responsibility. Maximize your area, and do not intrude on another person's area. If you are an usher, then usher, and let the parking lot attendant deal with traffic. If you are trying to do someone else's job, then you are probably not doing your own job the best you can.

When we are all in our places and doing our part, then the pastor can always trust everything is in order. He won't be thinking about anything but the congregation, and he will reach the pulpit ready to minister the Word of God unhindered by the responsibilities assumed by the ministry of helps.

ACTS 6:1-4

1 And in those days, when the number of the disciples was multiplied, there arose a murmuring of the Grecians against the Hebrews, because their widows were neglected in the daily ministration.

2 Then the twelve called the multitude of the disciples unto them, and said, It is not reason that we should leave the word of God, and serve tables.

3 Wherefore, brethren, look ye out among you seven men of honest report, full of the Holy Ghost and wisdom, whom we may appoint over this business.

4 But we will give ourselves continually to prayer, and to the ministry of the word.

The disciples were under direct order to take the Gospel to the world. They could not forsake the mandate of the Great Commission to serve tables. To solve the problem, they told the multitude to chose seven men of honest report who were filled with Holy Ghost and wisdom.

Today the pastor or minister should not have to stop flowing in the supernatural to handle natural ministry of helps situations. Just as in the Early Church, he should have faithful men and women who are of honest report and filled with the Holy Ghost and wisdom who will rally around him.

We need more men and women today in the Body of Christ who will hold up the minister's arms, so to speak, until the battle is won just as Aaron and Hur held Moses' arms up in Exodus 17:12. God wants faithful people to surround His ministers in order to make things easier for them to minister.

I have heard many preachers say that when they are physically tired, the anointing to minister to people is not as strong upon them. This fact alone should be enough to motivate us to serve in the helps ministry. If one of our loved ones had a serious need, we would want our pastor to be able to minister to him as effectively as possible.

If we do our part in the helps ministry, then the minister can minister to his flock the way the Lord intended. If the congregation would do their part and serve in the ministry of helps, then the pastor wouldn't wear himself out having to do his job *and* fulfill the congregation's responsibilities. Instead, he would be able minister to the needs of the people without being concerned about having enough nursery workers for the mid-week service or enough parking attendants to direct traffic on Sunday morning. It is a time- and energy-consuming chore for the pastor to beg and plead every week for help in these areas. He should be spending his time doing what he is supposed to do — ministering to his congregation.

ACTS 6:7

7   And the word of God increased; and the
number of the disciples multiplied in Jerusalem
greatly; and a great company of the priests were
obedient to the faith.

Because faithful men did their jobs waiting on
tables, many more souls were added to the Kingdom of
God. The disciples were able to continue fulfilling the
mandate of the Great Commission given to them by the
Head of the Church, the Lord Jesus Christ. When those
in the ministry of helps do their part and flow together
as a team, then the leaders can give themselves continually to the word of God and prayer.

Those Who Are Faithful Reap the Benefits

The Apostle Paul had many people who helped him
in the ministry. Many people, who aren't even mentioned
in the Bible by name, served Paul at very critical
moments. These people were willing to put their own
necks on the line for the man of God. We must realize
that sometimes the seemingly more feeble parts of the
Body of Christ make the greatest impact in critical
situations. The men and women who work behind the
scenes may never be known by name or be publicly
recognized by man, but they are just as necessary to
the Body of Christ as the public speaker. And, when
they serve faithfully, God takes note. God is the One
who will reward them openly.

GALATIANS 6:9

9   And let us not be weary in well doing: for
in due season we shall reap, if we faint not.

Whenever your "due season" comes, God will make sure everyone knows about it! He will bless your socks off for everyone to see! He will show the world the benefits that come with faithfully serving Him and His people.

Serving in the helps ministry will not only bless the Body of Christ, but it will benefit *you* as well. If you sense a call to the full-time ministry, you need to be involved in the ministry of helps right now. Remember, God is a God of order (1 Cor. 14:40). A person doesn't get saved one day and pastor a church the next day. So if your heart's desire is to work in full-time ministry, begin proving yourself faithful right now in the area of helps. There are benefits for being faithful!

I worked in a grocery store for several years before going into the ministry. I went through several levels of position before I became a manager. But having gone through those positions, I knew the details of all the different jobs. So when I was the manager and someone came to me saying he needed more time to stock a certain section, I knew from experience how much time it really took to stock it. If someone told me they couldn't mop the store in twenty minutes, I knew better, because I had mopped it hundreds of times in twenty minutes.

One benefit of being faithful in the ministry of helps is that when we enter the ministry position God has called us to, we can look back at our experiences in the helps positions. We will know what it takes to get the job done, and we will be able to teach and encourage others who are presently in the helps ministry.

The disciples trained with Jesus in His ministry before they ever had their own ministries. It is impossible to be successful in your own ministry without first having served in the ministry of helps, because God rewards faithfulness (Matt. 25:21). If you are faithful in small responsibilities such as setting up chairs, working with children, cleaning toilets, or singing in the choir, then God will add more responsibilities to you such as running the bookstore or being an usher captain.

You see, when you serve in the helps ministry, you are planting seed for your own ministry. God will reward your faithful service by sending people to serve you faithfully. That is why it is vitally important to take care of another man's time and materials as though they were your own. You *will* reap what you sow. If you sow bad seed into someone else's ministry, you will reap bad seed into your ministry. But if you sow good seed into someone else's ministry, you will reap good seed into your own.

1 CORINTHIANS 15:58

58 Therefore, my beloved brethren, be ye stedfast, unmoveable, always abounding in the work of the Lord, forasmuch as ye know that your labour is not in vain in the Lord.

As you work for the Lord, be creative in your area of responsibility. Believe God for new ideas. Never take any task, job, or responsibility lightly. Give your all every time you serve in the helps ministry, and God will reward your effort. If you are ushering, strive to have the best-looking section in the church. If you are a nursery worker, strive to be the biggest blessing to the kids. If you are a parking lot attendant, direct traffic with the joy of the Lord. If you are a sound engineer, have the best acoustics around. If you are a greeter, greet everyone with a smile. If you are a custodian, have the cleanest church in town.

COLOSSIANS 3:17

17 And whatsoever ye do in word or deed, do all in the name of the Lord Jesus, giving thanks to God and the Father by him.

In serving, we should do everything as though we were serving the Lord Jesus Himself. When our motive is to serve the Lord, we will do everything to the best of our ability.

Are You *Profitable*?

Can your pastor or leader say the same words about you that Paul said about Mark in Second Timothy 4:11?

2 TIMOTHY 4:11

11 Only Luke is with me. Take Mark, and bring him with thee: for he is PROFITABLE TO ME FOR THE MINISTRY.

Are you profitable to your pastor, organization, or church? We should all be profitable to our leaders. We are considered profitable when we faithfully serve and go out of our way to help those on the "front line" of ministry. For example, when missionaries come home to visit, we should hold them in high regard, because they are on the front line preaching the Gospel of Jesus Christ. We should endeavor to be a blessing to them in any way possible.

The Bible names several men and women who were profitable to their local church and to the Apostle Paul.

ROMANS 16:1,2

1 I commend unto you Phebe our sister, which is a servant of the church which is at Cenchrea:

2 That ye receive her in the Lord, as becometh saints, and that ye assist her in whatsoever business she hath need of you: for she hath been a succourer of many, and of myself also.

Phebe was profitable to her local church and to the Apostle Paul. She served in the ministry of helps and was highly regarded by others. Paul said she was a succourer. The Greek word translated "succourer" in this passage is "prostatis." "Prostatis" is the feminine form of the title given to a citizen in Athens who had the responsibility of seeing to the welfare of resident aliens who were without civic rights. Among the Jews, it signified a wealthy patron of the community. In other words, Phebe was a protector of people. She took care of those who were less fortunate or unable to take care of themselves. She was a great blessing to the people in Cenchrea. She was also a servant to the Apostle Paul and a servant of the Most High God.

Romans chapter 16 also mentions the husband and wife team of Priscilla and Aquila, who were both profitable to Paul.

ROMANS 16:3,4

3 Greet Priscilla and Aquila, my helpers in Christ Jesus:

4 Who have for my life laid down their own necks: unto whom not only I give thanks, but also all the churches of the Gentiles.

Priscilla and Aquila were members of the Early Church who risked their own necks for the Apostle Paul. They loved the Lord so much that they risked their lives for the furtherance of the Gospel. The Church today needs more people as faithful as Priscilla and Aquila — people who will do whatever is necessary so that the Gospel can be proclaimed.

TITUS 3:14

14 And let ours also learn to maintain good works for necessary uses, that they be not unfruitful.

We should always maintain a life of good works so that we will be profitable and fruitful to our leaders and to the Body of Christ.

CHAPTER 4

Serving in the Workplace

We have seen how we can serve in our everyday life and how we can serve God though serving people. We also studied how the ministry of helps serves the Body of Christ. Now let's look at serving in the workplace.

We should give one hundred percent effort every time we punch the time clock and be zealous about our work, like bees making honey. We need to do our jobs just as if the Lord Jesus Himself signed our paychecks. Someone might say, "But I don't like my job. I'm only there because the money is good." Regardless, God still expects our best performance.

If someone isn't giving his best effort when he doesn't like his job, he won't give his best effort even when he gets a job he likes. You see, it is not a matter of liking what you are doing; it is a matter of being ethical. Ethics is a matter of the heart.

EPHESIANS 6:5-7 (*The Amplified Bible*)

5 Servants (slaves), be obedient to those who are your physical masters, having respect for them and eager concern to please them, in singleness of motive and with all your heart, as [service] to Christ [Himself] —

6 Not in the way of eye-service [as if they were watching you] and only to please men, but as servants (slaves) of Christ, doing the will of God heartily and with your whole soul;

7 Rendering service readily with goodwill, as to the Lord and not to men.

When you respect your employer according to God's Word, you put yourself in a position for God to bless you.

Second Thessalonians 3:10 says, *"For even when we were with you, this we commanded you, that if any would not work, neither should he eat."* Christians should never be known as lazy people, because we have too much work to do! Jesus said that the harvest is plenteous but the laborers are few (Matt. 9:37). We have enough work to do to last us *two* lifetimes. So let's get busy.

COLOSSIANS 3:22-24

22 Servants, obey in all things your masters according to the flesh; not with eyeservice, as menpleasers; but in singleness of heart, fearing God:

23 And whatsoever ye do, do it heartily, as to the Lord, and not unto men;

24 Knowing that of the Lord ye shall receive the reward of the inheritance: for ye serve the Lord Christ.

We should give it our all every time we walk through the door at our place of employment. We shouldn't hold anything back or keep anything in reserve.

When I played high school football, my coach used to tell the team to leave everything we had on the practice field. Instead of practicing at half-speed, we were expected to give our best effort. My coach said, "The level at which you practice is the level at which you perform. If you play half-speed during practice, you will play half-speed during the game."

The same is true in life. Whatever we put into something, is what we are going to get out of it. We need to give our all — all the time. At the end of the day, we need to be able to say with a clear conscience, "I gave it my all today."

Our goal should be to be the best employee our company has ever had. We should punch the time clock at the end of the day the same way a person running a race reaches for the tape at the finish line. We please God by doing everything as unto Him — with all our heart and soul and strength.

Joseph — Egypt's Employee of the Month

We can learn how to be our company's greatest employee by studying the life of Joseph.

GENESIS 39:1-6

1   And Joseph was brought down to Egypt; and Potiphar, an officer of Pharaoh, captain of the guard, an Egyptian, bought him of the hands of the Ishmeelites, which had brought him down thither.

2   And the Lord was with Joseph, and he was a prosperous man; and he was in the house of his master the Egyptian.

3   And his master saw that the Lord was with him, and that the Lord made all that he did to prosper in his hand.

4   And Joseph found grace in his sight, and he served him: and he made him overseer over his house, and all that he had he put into his hand.

5   And it came to pass from the time that he had made him overseer in his house, and over all that he had, that the Lord blessed the Egyptian's house for Joseph's sake; and the blessing of the Lord was upon all that he had in the house, and in the field.

6   And he left all that he had in Joseph's hand; and he knew not ought he had, save the bread which he did eat. And Joseph was a goodly person, and well favoured.

Even though Joseph was sold into slavery by his own brothers, he kept in close fellowship with the Lord. Genesis 39:2 tells us that Joseph was prosperous, successful, and favored because the Lord was with him.

If we want to be successful in life, we must maintain a right relationship with the Lord. That means we are to put Him first in everything. Because Joseph kept God first in his life, he never became bitter with his brothers for betraying him. Nor did Joseph become bitter with the Lord for allowing the situation to happen.

Unfortunately, when many Christians go through a test or trial, they get upset with the Lord. They start questioning Him and wondering why certain things happened. But we need to remember that in some

instances, God will not deliver us *from* the trials of life —
He will take us *through* them. He will be right by our
side guiding us through to the other side and to victory!

When Potiphar saw that the Lord was with Joseph
and that the Lord made everything Joseph did to prosper, he made Joseph the overseer over his home.
Potiphar took all that belonged to him and put it into
Joseph's hands. In the same way, when you put God
first and serve Him faithfully, your coworkers and
supervisors will be able see the Lord in your life and in
your work. The work of your hands will be blessed, and
everything you touch will prosper. Every project you
work on will be a success, and those around you will
take notice.

Genesis 39:5 tells us that Joseph was made the
head of Potiphar's house. Joseph went from being a
slave to being the supervisor of Potiphar's house and
all of his possessions. The moment Joseph took over,
the Lord made everything Potiphar had to prosper. The
Lord can shake Wall Street because of one faithful servant! And God can turn a company around and make it
prosper just because of you!

Can Your Employer Trust You?

The Bible says Potiphar left all that he had in
Joseph's hand (Gen. 39:6). Can your employer leave all
that he has in your hands? Can he trust you with the
finances of the company? Can you be trusted to not
take the company's supplies home? If you have a deep-
rooted relationship with the Lord and if God has first
place in your life, then you should be able to answer
"yes" to these questions.

Joseph could be trusted by Potiphar, and Christians should be responsible enough to be trusted by their employers.

One day many years ago at the grocery store where I worked, the store manager was looking for a stock crew manager to be responsible for managing the crew who stocked the store after hours. The store manager asked me if I wanted the job. I told him no. I explained to him that I said no only because I understood the responsibility that went along with the position. That explanation got me hired for the job I didn't want. You see, he made me the stock manager because he liked the fact that I saw the responsibility of the position instead of the prestige and the privileges of the promotion.

Your employer and Potiphar should have one thing in common: They should not have to look after the company when you are around. When you are on the job, the boss or owner should be able to sleep at night. They should know that you will do your job and take care of the company just as well or better than they would themselves. They should be able to leave at a moment's notice without the company missing a beat. The company should stay on the course of success with you at the helm.

GENESIS 39:7-9
    7 And it came to pass after these things, that his master's wife cast her eyes upon Joseph; and she said, Lie with me.
    8 But he refused, and said unto his master's wife, Behold, my master wotteth not what is with me in the house, and he hath committed all that he hath to my hand;

9   There is none greater in this house than
I; neither hath he kept back any thing from me
but thee, because thou art his wife: how then
can I do this great wickedness, and sin against
God?

When the opportunity to sin presented itself to
Joseph, his dedication and commitment to the Lord
meant more to him than a few minutes of pleasure. If
you are tempted to sin by being lazy on the job, will
your commitment to the Lord mean more to you than a
few minutes of relaxation? If you know you got paid for
a forty-hour week when you only worked thirty-seven
hours, will you do the right thing and have your check
reissued for the right amount of hours? When you are
tempted to take an extra break without permission,
will your love for the Lord mean more to you in that
moment? Again, if you have a deep-rooted relationship
with the Lord, it will be no problem for you to resist the
opportunity to sin.

GENESIS 39:20-23

20 And Joseph's master took him, and put
him into the prison, a place where the king's
prisoners were bound: and he was there in the
prison.

21 But the Lord was with Joseph, and
shewed him mercy, and gave him favour in the
sight of the keeper of the prison.

22 And the keeper of the prison committed
to Joseph's hand all the prisoners that were in
the prison; and whatsoever they did there, he
was the doer of it.

23 The keeper of the prison looked not to any thing that was under his hand; because the Lord was with him, and that which he did, the Lord made it to prosper.

Potiphar's wife lied about Joseph and caused him to go to prison. But Joseph continued living as a faithful servant to the Lord, and the Lord continued to bless him even while he was in prison! You see, God can still bless the work of your hands if you get transferred to another department or to another state. It doesn't matter where you go, God can still make you a success. He will still bless the work of your hands, because He is God and He loves you!

In Genesis chapter 40, Joseph interpreted a dream for both the Pharaoh's butler and the Pharaoh's baker (vv. 3-19). When the butler was released from prison, he forgot about Joseph. But *God* did not forget about Joseph. God preserved Him, and two years later, Joseph was released from prison.

God will never leave you hanging. God said He would never leave you nor forsake you (Heb. 13:5)! He will always be there to bail you out of trouble. God always makes a way for His servants so they can keep serving Him.

God Makes a Way
Where There Is No Way!

God will always make a way for His people. It doesn't matter how hopeless your situation appears; God will make a way of escape for you. Our God specializes in impossible situations. Remember, there is nothing too big for the Lord to handle.

1 CORINTHIANS 10:13

**13 There hath no temptation taken you but
such as is common to man: but God is faithful,
who will not suffer you to be tempted above
that ye are able; but will with the temptation
also MAKE A WAY TO ESCAPE, that ye may be
able to bear it.**

I remember when I was kid in grade school. Any
time there was a fight, someone would always say, "I'm
going to get my big brother." I have carried this philos-
ophy into my adult life. Anytime I have a conflict with
the devil, I tell him I am going to get *my* Big Brother —
Jesus Christ! Jesus always takes care of the problem.

It does not matter how impossible the situation
looks. God gets excited about delivering His people
from impossible situations. In Acts chapter 12, God
made a way of escape for His servant Peter when it
seemed as though there was no way out. God delivered
Peter from death row! The Bible tells us that Peter was
kept under lock and key. He was guarded by sixteen
soldiers at all times and chained between two addi-
tional soldiers as he slept awaiting execution. Herod
wanted to kill Peter with a passion, but God had different plans. And God miraculously delivered Peter off
death row and out of the hands of Herod.

ACTS 12:11

**11 And when Peter was come to himself, he
said, Now I know of a surety, that the Lord hath
sent his angel, and hath delivered me out of the
hand of Herod, and from all the expectation of
the people of the Jews.**

If I were Peter, I would *still* be dancing and shout-
ing! Peter set a good example of how we should act in

the middle of a crisis. Peter knew he couldn't lose one way or the other. If God set him free, he would be free to continue preaching the Gospel. If he was executed the next day, he would be with Jesus in Heaven! So Peter just "rested in the arms of the Lord."

We should respond the same way in times of trouble. God is our Deliverer, and it doesn't matter what the doctor's report says or what the bank account looks like, God can make a way where there is no way!

God made a way for Mary and Martha when their brother Lazarus died. Lazarus had been dead for four days. Mary and Martha were in a great crisis. They were faced with a impossible situation. But Jesus went beyond the crisis. He went beyond impossibility. The power of God penetrated time, death, and the grave, and brought Lazarus back to life (John 11:43,44).

God can penetrate cancer, heart trouble, kidney trouble, and every other type of trouble. The mighty power of God can destroy every yoke of bondage!

God made a way where there was no way for His servant Moses and children of Israel at the Red Sea. After Moses led the Israelites out of Egypt, he stood with the Red Sea in front of him, several thousand people counting on him, and the angry Egyptian army closing in on him. Exodus 14:10 says, *"And when Pharaoh drew nigh, the children of Israel lifted up their eyes, and, behold, the Egyptians marched after them; and they were sore afraid: and the children of Israel CRIED OUT UNTO THE LORD."*

Sometimes when you are in the middle of a crisis, all you can do is cry out to the Lord. That's okay. Just remember to hang on, because your help is on the way!

As someone once said, "The Lord may not come when you want Him to, but He is *always* right on time!"

In Exodus 14:13, Moses told the children of Israel, "Fear not! Stand still, and see the salvation of the Lord!" The Lord told Moses stretch out his rod over the Red Sea, and Israel walked to the other side on dry land. Our God specializes in impossible situations. When you feel as though you are facing a sea of problems in your own life, remember that the Lord can make a way. When He comes on the scene, you will walk on dry land over to the side of victory!

God will always make a way for you when you serve Him — no matter how bad or impossible your situation seems. Luke 1:37 says, *"For with God nothing shall be impossible,"* so take courage. You are on your way out!

God Made a Way for Joseph

In Genesis chapter 41, Pharaoh dreamed a dream which eventually became Joseph's way out of prison.

GENESIS 41:15,16

15 And Pharaoh said unto Joseph, I have dreamed a dream, and there is none that can interpret it: and I have heard say of thee, that thou canst understand a dream to interpret it.

16 And Joseph answered Pharaoh, saying, It is not in me: God shall give Pharaoh an answer of peace.

Even though Joseph wanted to be delivered from prison, he did not try to take credit for having the gift to interpret dreams. He gave all the glory to God. In verse 16, Joseph told Pharaoh it was not his ability but God's. This really reveals that Joseph had a servant's heart. He did not try to exalt himself before Pharaoh.

Instead, he humbled himself and let God exalt him. God made Joseph the number-one man in the land. That's a big change from sitting in prison!

GENESIS 41:39,40

39 And Pharaoh said unto Joseph, Forasmuch as God hath shewed thee all this, there is none so discreet and wise as thou art:

40 Thou shalt be over my house, and according unto thy word shall all my people be ruled: only in the throne will I be greater than thou.

Joseph was now the number-one man in all the land of Egypt. God promoted him to the place where He want him to be. Even though Joseph was the ruler of Egypt next to Pharaoh, he remained a very hard worker. Often when an person gets promoted to a higher position, he slows down or gets a "big head" and starts to lord it over people.

When we are promoted, we must remember our commitment to the Lord to be a servant to Him and to people. Joseph stayed steadfast in serving people. He worked just as hard as he had worked before he was promoted.

GENESIS 41:48,49

48 And he [Joseph] gathered up all the food of the seven years, which were in the land of Egypt, and laid up the food in the cities: the food of the field, which was round about every city, laid he up in the same.

49 And Joseph gathered corn as the sand of the sea, very much, until he left numbering; for it was without number.

Joseph continued to serve and work in Egypt. He was faithful in serving, and the Lord lifted him up and honored him.

CHAPTER 5

Serving in the Fivefold Ministry

"Moreover it is required in stewards, that a man be found faithful."

— 1 Corinthians 4:2

No matter where we are in life, we must remember to be faithful to serve God and to serve people. Faithfulness is one of the most important ingredients in the success of anyone's life and ministry. If a person is not faithful, he will not be very successful at anything. Faithfulness doesn't start when we've reached the top, so to speak. Faithfulness starts in the little things. The Bible says that if we are faithful over the little God gives us, He will make us rulers over much (Matt. 25:21, Luke 19:17).

Every Christian is called to be a faithful servant — even those in full-time ministry. Unfortunately, most people don't consider the men and women in the five-fold ministry as servants. But when they are ministering to people, they are serving people. They are serving people every time they counsel, pray for the sick, or deliver someone from oppression. We may use different terminology to describe their service, but when you really break it down, they are serving people. Serving people is what being a minister is all about.

The Spirit of God was upon Jesus to minister and to serve. As I mentioned in Chapter 2, Jesus went about doing good things for people. If you're in the ministry, you should be doing good things for people by serving them.

LUKE 4:18,19
18 The Spirit of the Lord is upon me, because he hath anointed me to preach the gospel to the poor; he hath sent me to heal the brokenhearted, to preach deliverance to the captives, and recovering of sight to the blind, to set at liberty them that are bruised,
19 To preach the acceptable year of the Lord.

Preaching the Gospel to the poor, healing the brokenhearted, and preaching deliverance to the captives are good things and acts of serving. Preaching recovering of sight to the blind, setting at liberty them who are bruised, and preaching the acceptable year of the Lord are good things and acts of serving. These are the good things that we should be doing as we follow in Jesus' footsteps and live a life of service.

Servant by Day — Minister by Night

The Body of Christ needs more people who are willing to serve *and* to minister. For example, we need men and women who can serve tables *and* intercede for the saints. We need people who can clean toilets during the day and cast out devils at night. We need believers who can have a career during the day and hold evangelistic crusades at night.

We need servants like Philip who was chosen to wait on tables in Acts chapter 6 and who later went to Samaria and won the whole city for God!

ACTS 8:5-8

5 Then Philip went down to the city of Samaria, and preached Christ unto them.

6 And the people with one accord gave heed unto those things which Philip spake, hearing and seeing the miracles which he did.

7 For unclean spirits, crying with loud voice, came out of many that were possessed with them: and many taken with palsies, and that were lame, were healed.

8 And there was great joy in that city.

Philip is just one New Testament example of the kind of servant I am talking about.

We also need more servants like the Apostle Paul. He worked with his hands making tents, preached the Gospel, ministered to people, *and* wrote two-thirds of the New Testament.

ACTS 19:11,12

11 And God wrought special miracles by the hands of Paul:

12 So that from his body were brought unto the sick handkerchiefs or aprons, and the diseases departed from them, and the evil spirits went out of them.

Handkerchiefs or aprons filled with the power of God were taken from Paul's body to be laid on the sick and the demon-possessed. And when the cloths touched the oppressed, they were healed, delivered, and made whole!

We need more servants like Peter. In Acts chapter 6, he helped bring peace to a situation by appointing men to wait on tables, and in Acts chapter 9 he raised someone from the dead.

ACTS 9:40
40 But Peter put them all forth, and kneeled down, and prayed; and turning him to the body said, Tabitha, arise. And she opened her eyes: and when she saw Peter, she sat up.

God worked mighty wonders through Peter. But Peter's willingness to serve came long before the signs and wonders.

The Purpose of Ministry
Is Still To Serve

God gave the fivefold-ministry gifts to the Body of Christ for the purpose of serving people. We should love, honor, and respect our pastors and spiritual leaders because they look out for our well being. Hebrews 13:17 says, *"Obey them that have the rule over you, and submit yourselves: for they watch for your souls, as they that must give account, that they may do it with joy, and not with grief: for that is unprofitable for you."* The Lord placed the ministry gifts in the Body of Christ to bless the Church. Ministers have the tremendous responsibility of perfecting the saints for the work of the ministry.

EPHESIANS 4:8-16
8 Wherefore he saith, When he ascended up on high, he led captivity captive, and gave gifts unto men.

9 (Now that he ascended, what is it but that he also descended first into the lower parts of the earth?

10 He that descended is the same also that ascended up far above all heavens, that he might fill all things.)

11 And he gave some, apostles; and some, prophets; and some, evangelists; and some, pastors and teachers;

12 For the perfecting of the saints, for the work of the ministry, for the edifying of the body of Christ:

13 Till we all come in the unity of the faith, and of the knowledge of the Son of God, unto a perfect man, unto the measure of the stature of the fulness of Christ:

14 That we henceforth be no more children, tossed to and fro, and carried about with every wind of doctrine, by the sleight of men, and cunning craftiness, whereby they lie in wait to deceive;

15 But speaking the truth in love, may grow up into him in all things, which is the head, even Christ:

16 From whom the whole body fitly joined together and compacted by that which every joint supplieth, according to the effectual working in the measure of every part, maketh increase of the body unto the edifying of itself in love.

As ministers, we should look forward to serving the souls God has entrusted to our care. There is no higher honor in the world than the honor of serving God's people.

In First Timothy 3:1, the Apostle Paul said, *"This is a true saying, If a man desire the office of a bishop, he desireth a good work."* Paul referred to the ministry as being *good work.* Serving God's people is good work. If a person doesn't want to serve people, then he should not pursue being in the ministry. You see, preaching is the one of the easiest parts of the ministry. But the preacher must be willing to pay the price and *serve* the people of God.

Biblical Examples of Faithful Ministers

Lets look in the Word of God at some more ministers in the Early Church who ministered *for* the Lord and *to* the Lord through their faithful acts of service.

Epaphroditus

Epaphroditus is one example of a faithful minister.

PHILIPPIANS 2:24-30

24 But I trust in the Lord that I also myself shall come shortly.

25 Yet I supposed it necessary to send to you Epaphroditus, my brother, and companion in labour, and fellowsoldier, but your messenger, and he that ministered to my wants.

26 For he longed after you all, and was full of heaviness, because that ye had heard that he had been sick.

27 For indeed he was sick nigh unto death: but God had mercy on him; and not on him only, but on me also, lest I should have sorrow upon sorrow.

**28 I sent him therefore the more carefully,
that, when ye see him again, ye may rejoice,
and that I may be the less sorrowful.**

**29 Receive him therefore in the Lord with
all gladness; and hold such in reputation:**

**30 Because for the work of Christ he was
nigh unto death, not regarding his life, to sup-
ply your lack of service toward me.**

Epaphroditus was a faithful brother in the ministry.
He always did whatever was necessary to get the job
done. Epaphroditus was a great blessing to Paul's ministry and to Paul personally. He didn't hesitate to offer
his life in service for the Kingdom.

We need more people like Epaphroditus in the Body
of Christ — those who will go through the fire and back
again. We need those who will not run away when the
pressure is on or when it looks as though everything
has gone wrong. We need those who will risk their lives
for the Gospel's sake. Men and women of this caliber
are hard to find these days, but there are still some
people with character who will stand up and be counted
in the Body of Christ.

Judas and Silas

Judas (not Iscariot) and Silas were two men in the
fivefold ministry who were always busy serving the
people of God.

ACTS 15:25-27

**25 It seemed good unto us, being assembled
with one accord, to send chosen men unto you
with our beloved Barnabas and Paul,**

26 Men that have hazarded their lives for the name of our Lord Jesus Christ.

27 We have sent therefore Judas and Silas, who shall also tell you the same things by mouth.

The Early Church could count on Judas and Silas. They were ministers who risked their lives for the sake of the Gospel. Serving God's people meant everything to them, and they were committed to God's service. Because they served God and served people, Judas and Silas were both a tremendous blessing to the Body of Christ.

Remember, as ministers we are still called to be servants of the people. Every apostle, prophet, evangelist, pastor, and teacher should be known first and foremost as a servant of the people. There is no higher calling than that of being a servant. And although there will never be a greater Servant than our Lord and Savior Jesus Christ, we must always strive to follow the example He set for us.

CHAPTER 6

Giving Honor to Whom Honor Is Due

"Render therefore to all their dues: tribute to whom tribute is due; custom to whom custom; fear to whom fear; honour to whom honour."

— Romans 13:7

Being a minister of the Gospel myself, I believe *every* minister should honor the people who serve in the ministry of helps. We should not look down upon or take for granted anyone who works for us. Without the men and women who faithfully serve in the ministry of helps, full-time ministers would never fulfill the vision God has given them. The people in the ministry of helps and those who are not called to the fivefold ministry are very essential to the Body of Christ. And most of our thanks should go to the people who help and serve us.

Everyone wants to feel loved and appreciated, and everyone needs a pat on the back once in a while. We should honor the people who make us successful in our ministries and careers. And we should always try our best to not be partial or to esteem one person higher than another. Everyone is very important and very necessary. There is no big "I" and little "you" when it comes to doing the work of the Lord. We are all members of the same Body of Christ (1 Cor. 12:12-27), and we are all servants of the Most High God.

I would like to honor the unnamed individuals who served with the Apostle Paul in the Book of Acts. Without their help, Paul would not have been able to do what God had called him to do. These men and women served God by serving the Apostle Paul. Some of them even risked their lives to save his.

Honoring Unsung Heroes

- The disciples who let Paul down the wall in Damascus to escape from the Jews who wanted to kill him (Acts 9:23-25).

- The brethren who brought Paul down to Caesarea to escape from the Grecians who wanted to kill him (Acts 9:29,30).

- The men in Paul's company who sailed with him from Paphos to Perga in Pamphylia and then to Antioch (Acts 13:13-14).

- Those who made Paul aware of the sacrifices the priest and the people were planning to make to honor Paul and Barnabas as gods. Because Paul was told of their plans, he was able to stop them (Acts 14:13-18).

- The disciples who came to Paul's side after he was stoned (Acts 14:20).

- The Church at Jerusalem, the apostle, and the elders who received Paul and his company on their way back from Antioch (Acts 15:4).

- The jailer who, after he received the Lord, washed Paul's stripes, took him to his home, fed him, and gave him the message that the chief priest was going to let him go (Acts 16:33-36).

- The brethren who sent Paul by night to Berea to escape from the Jews in Thessalonica (Acts 17:5-10).

- The brethren who sent Paul away from Berea when the Jews from Thessalonica followed him there. (Acts 17:14).

- The brethren who took Paul to Athens and carried a message from Paul to Silas and Timotheus (Acts 17:15).

- The people who brought handkerchiefs and aprons to be placed on Paul's body and then took them to be placed on the sick (Acts 19:12).

- The disciples who would not let Paul enter the theater in Ephesus because of the present danger (Acts 19:30).

- The important person in Asia who was a friend of Paul and told him not to go into the theater because of the present danger (Acts 19:31).

- The brothers who met Paul and took him in the ship at Assos and went with him to Mitylene (Acts 20:13-14).

- The elders who traveled from Miletus to Ephesus when Paul called for them (Acts 20:17-18).

- All the believers who walked with Paul until they were out of the city and then kneeled down and prayed with him on the shore (Acts 21:5).

- The brethren who gladly received Paul at Jerusalem (Acts 21:17).

- The four men who went with Paul to the temple to signify the completion of the days of purification (Acts 21:26).

- Paul's nephew who told him about the conspiracy to kill him (Acts 23:12-16).

- The brethren at Puteoli who asked Paul to tarry with them for seven days (Acts 28:14).

- The brethren who heard Paul was in the area and traveled as far as Appiiforum to meet him (Acts 28:15).

I pray this book has inspired and motivated you to serve. I want to leave you with this question: If being a servant was a crime, would there be enough evidence to convict you? Remember, it is more blessed to serve than to be served. May God bless you always as you follow in the steps of the greatest Servant of all — Jesus Christ.

About the Author

Rev. Byron August was born in 1964 in Donaldsonville, Louisiana, and at the age of eight, he accepted Jesus Christ as his Savior. Inspired by his grandmother, Rev. August began a life of serving and has been very active in the helps ministry ever since.

When Rev. August was eighteen years old, he began attending a Full Gospel Church. Eager to embrace every opportunity to serve people, Rev. August performed janitorial duties, worked in the church bookstore, and visited nursing homes and jails. After proving faithful to serve, he was appointed to oversee various areas of the church's helps ministry and outreach programs. In addition to these duties, Rev. August also taught a Sunday School class and served as a deacon in the church.

In 1984, Rev. August graduated from Nicholls State University in Thibodaux, Louisiana, with an Associate of Science in general business. In 1988, Rev. August answered the call to full-time ministry and enrolled at RHEMA Bible Training Center in Broken Arrow, Oklahoma. He graduated in 1990.

Rev. August began working as an employee at Kenneth Hagin Ministries in 1988. In 1992, he took a sixteen-month sabbatical to serve as a missionary to Lima, Peru, South America. While on the mission field, Rev. August ministered in various churches throughout the country, taught in a local Bible school, and worked in a local missions station.

Rev. August is a licensed itinerant minister who conducts services throughout the United States and Latin America.